Petersen, Palle
   Boy in Bangladesh.
   1. Dacca, Bangladesh – Social life and customs –
Juvenile literature
   I. Title   II. Forlag, Borgens
   954.9'22   DS396.9.D3

   ISBN 0-7136-2119-2

First published in English by A & C Black (Publishers) Limited
35 Bedford Row, London WC1R 4JH
Original Danish edition published by Borgens Forlag, Copenhagen
with the title *Ali er Kuli*
© 1977 Palle Petersen
© 1981 (English text) A & C Black (Publishers) Ltd.
Reprinted 1983
Acknowledgments
The maps are by Tony Garrett
The photographs are by Palle Petersen except for page 16 which is by Politikens
Pressefoto (Denmark)

Filmset by August Filmsetting, Reddish, Stockport
Printed and bound in Great Britain by
William Clowes (Beccles) Limited, Beccles and London

Boy in Bangladesh

Palle Petersen

Adam & Charles Black
London

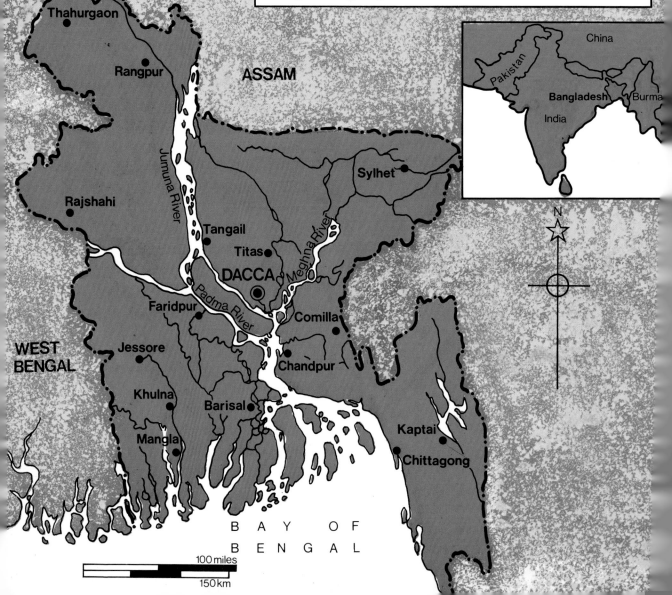

Shahid is eleven years old and he lives in Bangladesh. If you look at the map, you can see that Bangladesh is to the north-east of India, between the states of West Bengal and Assam. Bangladesh is about the same size as England and Wales.

The name Bangladesh means 'the country of the Bengalis'. Shahid is a Bengali. He speaks the Bangla language.

Shahid works as a porter in the market in Dacca. Dacca is the capital city of Bangladesh.

Shahid works with lots of other boys who are also porters. They are all friends. Their families are poor so the boys have to go out to work. There is only just enough work for them in the market, so they try to stop other boys working there. Shahid was only able to become a porter when another boy died and Shahid took his place.

Shahid waits for someone to give him a job.
Sometimes he waits all day and still doesn't get any
work. But today he is lucky – a man wants him to
carry his shopping. Shahid uses a big round basket
to carry the food.

The man picks the vegetables he wants and the seller weighs them on his scales. Then the vegetables are put in Shahid's basket. He carries the basket on his head, resting on a piece of cloth.

In Bangladesh, the men nearly always do the shopping. The women stay indoors. Bengalis are Muslims. Most of them believe that women should stay at home to look after the home and family.

Later on, the man buys a bowl of cooked rice from two children in the market. Shahid is hungry too, but he doesn't have any money. He must wait until the man pays him.

Lots of other children work in the market. Shahid knows most of them. These boys make pancakes and sell them. Shahid sometimes buys one if he has enough money.

One boy mixes the rice, flour and water into dough. Another boy uses a thin stick to roll out the dough into pancakes. Someone else fries them. The boys saved up for ages to buy a frying pan.

The two boys here work in the meat market. They have been hired to persuade people to buy meat. They stand in front of the meat stall and shout 'Cheap meat! Freshly killed oxen! Come and buy!'

Shahid hasn't eaten meat for a long time. He can hardly remember what it tastes like. He can only afford rice.

This is Abdul, a friend of Shahid's. He works in the market too. He earns money by polishing shoes. On a good day he polishes twenty pairs of shoes. Most of his customers are rich tourists or Bengalis who work in offices in Dacca.

Abdul's friend is called Mohammed. He mends punctures in bicycle tyres. Mohammed used to live in the country, but his parents died so he came to Dacca to look for work. Most people in Bangladesh live in the country.

Mohammed has only been in town for a few days so he hasn't found anywhere to live yet. He sleeps under some trees with other homeless boys.

Bengali money

Here are the coins and bank notes which are used in Bangladesh. The coins are called paisa and the notes are called taka. There are 100 paisa in a taka.

For one taka, you could buy a small bar of chocolate. A family like Shahid's, probably spends about 250 taka a month on food such as rice, fish, eggs and sometimes meat.

Paisa coins

1 Paisa   2 Paisa

5 Paisa   10 Paisa

25 Paisa   50 Paisa

Taka bank notes

At last, the man finishes his shopping and pays Shahid. On a good day, Shahid can earn more than a grown-up working in the market.

Shahid walks home with some of the other boys from the market. They are carrying fresh water to drink. Shahid has to go straight home to give his father the money he has earned. The money is used to buy food for the whole family. Shahid can't spend it himself.

Here is Shahid with his father and some friends.
His father has been out of work for two years. There
isn't much work in the city unless you have been to
school and can read and write. Shahid's money is
all the family has to live on.

Shahid's father is smoking a large pipe. He talks
with his friends about when the family lived in the
country. He can remember it well.

They weren't rich then, either, but there was nearly always enough to eat. They only had one small field, but it was big enough to provide rice for the whole family.

Every few months, the field was ploughed using two cows. Then it was planted with rice. Pipes from the nearby river carried water to the field. The sun made the rice grow quickly.

Three times a year, everyone helped to harvest the rice. Even the old people joined in. Scythes were used to cut the rice stalks and then the children gathered them into bundles. Machines and modern tractors are now being used much more.

Shahid's family used to live in a village by the river.
Nearly everybody in the country lives near a river
because they need the water.

The river is used for everything. People drink the
water and bathe in it. It is used to water the
animals and irrigate the crops.

The children liked playing in the river. They used to
take the cows down there to drink. Then they
played games and splashed each other.

Every summer, the monsoon comes. It rains for
three months, almost without stopping. The fields
are usually flooded, but that doesn't matter because
rice grows better with its roots in water, as long as
its leaves are in the sun.

Shahid's village was built on a hill so the houses
stayed dry inside when the rains came, even though
the footpaths were muddy.

Sometimes it rains even harder than usual. The
floods are so high that the rice is washed away.
There is no food. The water comes into the houses.
Whole villages are sometimes washed away, and
people and animals are drowned.

Shahid can remember when his village was flooded. Their cows were drowned and the rice crop was ruined. They sold their land to a rich farmer just to get enough money to buy food.

That was why the family decided to move to Dacca. They hoped they would find somewhere to live and that Shahid's father would get a job.

When they arrived in Dacca, they built a shelter from bamboo sticks. They were very poor. Two of Shahid's sisters died from disease. Shahid went to work in the market to earn money for the family.

Shahid became ill once, too. He had stomach ache, a temperature and he was sick. His parents were worried. There are still many dangerous diseases in Bangladesh and they were afraid Shahid might die.

Shahid's father took him to the government doctor. It didn't cost any money because the Bengali government pays for most of the medical care in Bangladesh. It is trying to wipe out serious diseases and starvation in the country.

The doctor examined Shahid. He said that Shahid had been drinking river water which had germs in it. He gave Shahid an injection and some pills to take. He was soon better.

Shahid has three brothers and two sisters. His parents would like more children. They could get jobs like Shahid and make the family richer. And they could look after their parents when they are old.

But the government wants to stop people having such large families. There are too many people and not enough food, jobs or houses in Bangladesh.

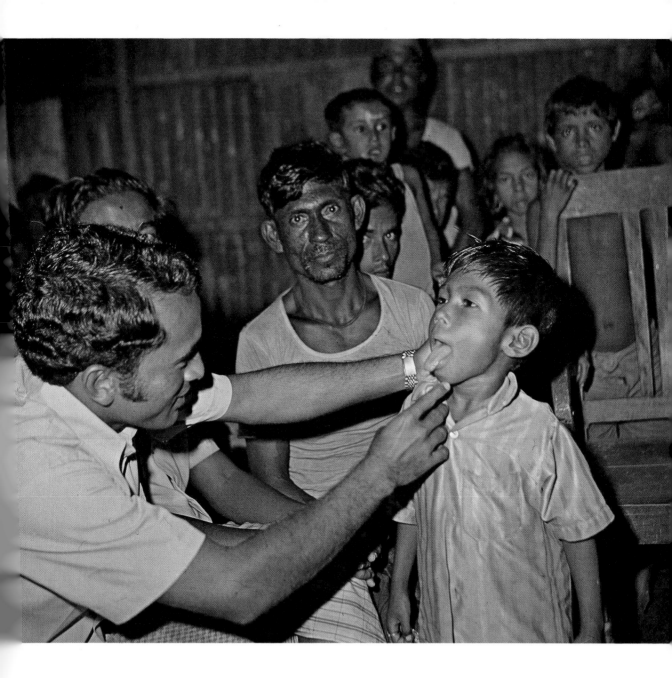

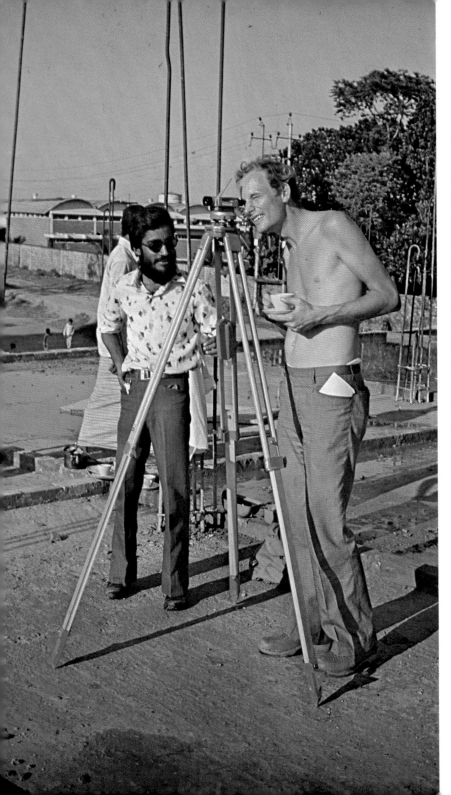

The government is also trying to develop the country's industries and improve the roads and railways. Foreign countries like Britain, Japan, West Germany and America send aid to Bangladesh to help the government do this.

Money and food is sent to Bangladesh. Technicians and engineers also visit the country to advise and train the Bengalis. Many Bengalis go to Britain to study so that they can return to their country and help to develop it.

But most people are still very poor. This is Shahid's cousin. Her husband is dead and she is alone with her child. No-one wants to marry her because she has already been married. She can't get a job because she has to look after her child.

So she has to beg. She never gets very much money. Usually just enough to buy a bowl of rice and some vegetables.

Shahid goes to school for just two hours each day. The rest of the time he must work in the market. He is learning to read and write. Soon he will be the only one in his family who can. Perhaps then he will be able to get a better job. He is often cheated at the market because he can't do arithmetic.

At school, Shahid also learns history and geography. He plays a lot of football. It is a very popular game in Bangladesh.

Most people in Bangladesh can't read or write. So the government, with foreign aid, is trying to improve education. More teachers are being trained and there are new books in the schools. Every child up to the age of ten has to go to primary school. It is free.

But parents still have to pay to send their children to secondary school. So it is usually only the children from rich families who go there. Secondary schools for poorer children, like Shahid, are now being built. Shahid's parents don't have to pay to send him to school.

Here is Shahid with some of his family. His mother is cooking rice for their supper.

Shahid works hard at school because he wants to get a better job and earn more money for his family. Perhaps then they won't have to worry too much about where their next meal is coming from.

The Bengali alphabet

এ	বি	সি	ডি	ই	এফ্	জি	এইচ	আই	জে	কে	এল	এম
A	B	C	D	E	F	G	H	I	J	K	L	M

এন	ও	পি	কিউ	আর	এস	টি	ইউ	ভি	ডব্লিউ	এক্স	ওয়াই	জেড
N	O	P	Q	R	S	T	U	V	W	X	Y	Z

Useful addresses for more information on Bangladesh:

Centre for World Development Education
128 Buckingham Palace Road
London SW1V 13S

Oxfam Education Department
274 Banbury Road
Oxford OX27 DZ

The Underprivileged Children's
Educational Programme
63, Road 12A
Dhanmondi RA
Dacca
Bangladesh

Information Office
Bangladesh High Commission
28 Queen's Gate
London SW7 5JA

Index